Taking part in uncertainty

Taking part in uncertainty

The significance of labour market and income protection reforms for social segmentation and citizens' discontent

J.C. Vrooman

The Netherlands Institute for Social Research | scp
Utrecht University
The Hague/Utrecht, July 2016

The Netherlands Institute for Social Research | scp was established by Royal Decree of March 30, 1973 with the following terms of reference:

a   to carry out research designed to produce a coherent picture of the state of social and cultural welfare in the Netherlands and likely developments in this area;
b   to contribute to the appropriate selection of policy objectives and to provide an assessment of the advantages and disadvantages of the various means of achieving those ends;
c   to seek information on the way in which interdepartmental policy on social and cultural welfare is implemented with a view to assessing its implementation.

The work of the Netherlands Institute for Social Research focuses especially on problems coming under the responsibility of more than one Ministry. As Coordinating Minister for social and cultural welfare, the Minister for Health, Welfare and Sport is responsible for the policies pursued by the Netherlands Institute for Social Research. With regard to the main lines of such policies the Minister consults the Ministers of General Affairs; Security and Justice; the Interior and Kingdom Relations; Education, Culture and Science; Finance; Infrastructure and the Environment; Economic Affairs, Agriculture and Innovation; and Social Affairs and Employment.

© The Netherlands Institute for Social Research | scp / J.C. Vrooman, 2016
scp-publication 2016-20
First published as *Meedoen in onzekerheid; verwachtingen over participatie en protectie*
Translated from the Dutch by Julian A. Ross, Carlisle, uk
dtp: Textcetera, The Hague
Cover design: bureau Stijlzorg, Utrecht
Cover picture: adaptation of a picture of Bert Kaufmann via Flickr
Author picture back cover: Robert Goddyn
Picture p. 50-51: Irma Schenk
isbn 978 90 377 0799 1

Distribution outside the Netherlands and Belgium: Transaction Publishers, New Brunswick (USA)

The Netherlands Institute for Social Research	scp	Utrecht University
P.O. Box 16164	po Box 80125
2500 bd Den Haag	3508 tc Utrecht
The Netherlands	The Netherlands
Tel. +31 70 340 70 00	
Website: www.scp.nl	
E-mail: info@scp.nl	

The authors of scp-publications can be contacted by e-mail via the scp-website.

Rector Magnificus,

Thank you for your introductory words.

Dear Colleagues, Family, Friends and Guests,

Today is a special day in several respects. It was only after I had fixed the date for this gathering today that I became aware that we are this week celebrating the 380th anniversary of the founding of Utrecht University. I was briefly tempted to dedicate my inaugural lecture to the celebration of that illustrious event, but in the end decided against doing so. It does however give me great pleasure to be delivering this lecture on such an auspicious day, in acceptance of my endowed professorship in the discipline of social security and participation. That pleasure is enhanced by a personal – and slightly intriguing – experience. However, I shall reserve that until the end of my lecture.

I never knew my grandparents on my father's side. Grandmother Magdalina died shortly after the Second World War, and after a while my grandfather Henk moved in with my young parents. As a self-employed person, he had not built up a pension. What assets he had evaporated as a result of the crisis in the 1930s and then the German Occupation. The start was difficult for this extended household. Today we might call them 'co-residents'. But such administrative labels, which frame our daily lives today, did not exist then; it was simply an accepted and usual thing to do. Luckily, grandfather Henk was eventually deemed to be eligible for a modest old-age pension. Although he was able to draw this pension for some years, sadly he died before I was born.

After the War, much of the Dutch economy, physical infrastructure and housing stock lay in ruins. Textiles and tobacco were rationed. The social security system was also in a deplorable state, and the situation regarding provision for old age was nothing short of acute. The benefits were meagre, and the combination of recession and war meant that those without insurance often had not been able to save enough for their final years. As a consequence, many older persons were forced to rely on their children for support; in many cases, as with my grandfather, this involved moving in with them. The situation was so precarious that it prompted the then Minister of Social Affairs, Willem Drees, to bring forward emergency legislation to provide for people in old age (the *Noodwet Ouderdomsvoorziening*). The new benefits scheme, introduced in 1947, was received enthusiastically.

In this image you can see a group of grateful older persons applauding Drees during a festive gathering to mark the introduction of the *Noodwet*, held in the Zoo in The Hague.

Spaarnestad Photo/National Archives of the Netherlands, through Wikimedia Commons

If we were to take a similar photograph today, it would probably look very different – not just because of the clothing and the sparse plainness of this photo, but also because of the way in which the subjects perceive their roles, their facial expressions and their interaction. The man with the glasses accompanying Willem Drees is Mr Van Beek, the president of the body which represented older people at the time, the *Algemene Bond van*

Ouden van Dagen. He gives the impression that the responsibility of his role as host weighs heavily on him. As for Willem Drees, the taller figure in the centre of the picture, if he is aware of the camera at all, it is in a different way from a modern-day politician, who would no doubt be smiling broadly and glad-handing, because in the world of today's media that comes across as warmer and more human, and not as undignified. And last but not least, pensioners today would probably appear much less docile than those in this picture, and would most likely include a few migrants.

The gratitude of those older people is also evident from the many letters written to Drees by members of the public.[1] An example is a letter from a Mr Van Hooff from Eindhoven, in which he writes about the *Noodwet*:

> This is the greatest, most blessed work ever achieved in the Netherlands .... You will ... to all eternity have a place in our hearts, and we, the older generation, salute you. The undersigned ran a small self-employed business, worked hard but did not make enough to put aside any savings, and it is for that reason that I am so grateful to Your Excellency, for providing me with a little money in my 82nd year that I can spend as I see fit; because a person sometimes needs things, and it is moreover such a sad condition to have to beg for charity.

Sister Feliciane Jenkens, a nun from Amersfoort, wrote how Drees' *Noodwet* made her feel liberated:

> The fact that we are able to enjoy such a fine old age in our advanced years is thanks to you. Yours truly is a religious person who has now been given the opportunity to visit family occasionally, to do someone a favour, something that I could not even contemplate between the ages of 20 and 70.

And J. Raap from Amsterdam even spontaneously gave Drees something back in return for the benefit:

> [I feel] obliged to send a small gift in the form of a tobacco coupon [...] in appreciation of the fine thing that you have done for the older generation! In the vernacular it is said 'you will receive a chair in heaven'. For my part, you will receive four... in my thoughts!

Getting such letters of gratitude would be a rarity for a member of cabinet today. The ministry which was once led by Willem Drees now has a Communications Department, and within it a group of civil servants who are responsible for answering messages from the public. I recently asked whether the Minister or the State Secretary had received any thank-you letters or emails from members of the public in recent years for the policy they had pursued. The initial reaction of one information officer was to laugh at the very idea; but after a little thought, a colleague remembered that 'two such messages' had been received recently. However, she could not recall the thrust of these responses, and the emails themselves could not readily be found. The latter is not uncommon in The Hague...[2]

By contrast, there were plenty of examples of 'ungrateful' reactions, and the information officers were kind enough to send me a few anonymised quotes. One member of the public recently wrote the following about the 'co-resident rule', also referred to as the 'informal care tax':[3]

> How can a ministry bring in a law which means that the less well-off are driven into misery? [...] My son cannot afford to help with my housing costs, but nonetheless the benefit is simply cut by 250 euros. I call that inhuman. Since I have become aware of this, I have become severely depressed and no longer see the point in living.

Another wrote to the State Secretary:

> You are helping to create a society in which children are no longer able to take any responsibility for their parents. In my view, the informal care tax is extremely unwise: bad for the Netherlands, bad for the adult children affected and bad for the Labour Party. Many party members simply do not understand this lack of solidarity. I certainly do not.

And a third writer penned the following on the requirement to do something in return for receiving social assistance benefit:

> Under the new legislative proposals [...] the illiterate, foreigners and Frisians will be obliged to learn standard Dutch; people with tattoos or piercings, long hair or a mental health disorder will be obliged to behave in accordance with the norm; people will be forced to accept

unsuitable work. [...] Could you please explain to me how these measures can be reconciled with the Labour Party credo of 'Stronger and More Social'?

And these are fairly moderate reactions – Social Affairs and Employment Minister Lodewijk Asscher recently posted a number of responses from citizens on Facebook which were rather more extreme.[4]

The differences between the old 'grateful' and the present 'ungrateful' public reactions illustrate how radically expectations about social security have changed over time.[5] What lies behind this reversal? A few obvious explanations spring to mind:
— People today are better educated and more assertive than in the past;
— Modern communication tools mean it is easier, quicker and cheaper to express an opinion;
— The power elite is currently much more 'lonely' than in the 1940s and 1950s.[6]

All these factors undoubtedly play a role, but that is not what I wish to talk about today. Social security is an institutional system. Originally, it was intended to guarantee an acceptable minimum income and to enable living standards to be maintained to a certain degree when people face specific risks.[7] Those objectives have changed in recent decades, with policy focusing more and more on participation.[8] In this lecture I will explore to what extent the reversal in public reactions is linked to changes in the security of work and income. I will also look briefly at the relationship between social networks and benefit dependency, one of the central topics for this new Chair.

35 years of income security

Many people have the idea that income security in the Netherlands has been reducing steadily and steeply since the 1980s. With a nod to Raymond Chandler and Bruno Palier, this might be described as 'a long goodbye to Drees'.[9] That people have this impression is understandable:

social security regulations have undergone many changes over the last 35 years. A few examples will make this clear:
- The reduction and repeated non-indexation of the social minimum income;
- The changes to the duration and amount of the unemployment insurance benefit;
- The raising of the statutory retirement age;
- The rise and fall of early retirement and pre-pension schemes;
- The curtailment of surviving dependants' benefit;
- The changing stipulations in social assistance on applying for jobs, cohabiting, active reintegration and reciprocity;
- And the difficult transformation of the rules on sick leave and disability benefits.

All this has led to serious political tensions over the years and has inevitably had an impact on society.[10] But is the impression of steadily declining income security accurate? And if it is, how steep is that decline, and has everyone been affected by it to the same degree? To gain some insight into this, I performed a quantitative analysis of the institutional changes since 1980.[11] I looked at developments in statutory coverage, benefit conditions, benefit levels, benefit duration and reintegration for each individual risk – unemployment, old age, sick leave, and so on. All told, the analysis included 59 institutional characteristics, and I calculated annual ratings on a ten-point scale for each risk.[12] These figures were subsequently combined to obtain average annual income protection scores above and below retirement age.

For those aged under 65, we do indeed see a declining trend, but this did not begin until 1990 (Figure 1). During the 1980s, the overall income protection of the potential labour force improved somewhat. That was mostly due to the explosive growth in early retirement schemes and the amelioration of unemployment insurance benefit rights. The latter applied especially for older persons: the maximum benefit duration was extended, with a stronger link to people's employment history. In addition, the income protection score rose because a sizeable group of widowers became entitled to surviving dependant's benefit in 1988; before that

Figure 1   Income protection: social security (1980-2015)*

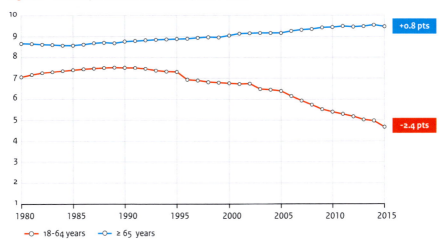

*   59 criteria (coverage, conditions, level, duration and re-integration) for (a) state retirement pension (AOW) and supplementary occupational pension; (b) benefit schemes for unemployment, sickness leave, disability, surviving dependants, early retirement/pre-pension, social assistance.

Sources: see Appendix 1

Figure 2   Income security of population aged 18+ (1980-2015; index scores, 1980=100)

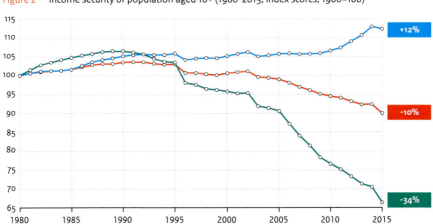

year, only widows and orphans were eligible for this scheme. Until 1990, the increased rights of those taking early retirement, older unemployed persons and widowers outstripped the curbs on social assistance and disability benefits.

From 1990 onwards, however, the trend turns downwards. Early retirement schemes and the special provisions for older unemployed persons were gradually phased out. Under the new General Surviving Dependants Act (*Algemene Nabestaandenwet*), men and women acquired equal rights – but those rights were equally limited. Further substantial reductions in entitlement were introduced in the social assistance and disability benefit schemes. The transfer of civil servants to the less generous employee insurance schemes also depressed the score. The introduction of the Participation Act (*Participatiewet*) in 2015 is the final element in this 25-year process of decline. It produces an additional kink in the graph.

What is striking is that, since the middle of the 1990s, there have been virtually no instances of an increase in the protection for people below retirement age. One exception is the extension of the sick leave scheme, which up to 2004 lasted a year. However, this did not cost the government any money: the obligation to continue paying a sick employee's wages for the first two years of their illness came to rest upon employers. There were also a number of small increases in benefit levels during the first months of unemployment insurance, and for the specific group of people with a full and permanent incapacity for work. Finally, the reintegration budgets rose from the mid-1990s, slightly countering the downward trend. However, that mitigating effect has since been cancelled out by the sharp cuts in recent years.

People of working age therefore did experience a 'long goodbye to Drees', but only from 1990 onwards. The change among this group was considerable: their income protection score fell from 7.1 in 1980 to 4.7 in 2015.

The picture is very different for retired persons. They already had a high score in 1980 (8.7), and this improved further over time to reach 9.5 in 2014 before falling back very slightly in the last measurement year. This positive trend among older people is due in the first place to the fact that more and more people had built up supplementary occupational pensions, which were also higher on average. In addition, rising life expectancy has meant that people receive their state and supplementary pensions for longer. Finally, the statutory minimum old age pensions have increased in real terms since the 1990s. After 2008 they rose above their 1980 level, whereas social assistance benefit levels in 2015 were still below that threshold.

The favourable general trend for older persons is mitigated somewhat by the fact that more and more people are seeing their statutory minimum pension cut because they have not lived in the Netherlands continuously prior to age 65.[13] In supplementary occupational pensions, the transition from final salary to average salary schemes has also imparted a downward effect, as has the raising of the statutory retirement age which began in 2015 – the same year in which the purchasing power of supplementary pensions fell due to non-indexation, and the state pension allowance for younger partners was abolished. Seen over the period as a whole, however, there has been no question of a 'long goodbye to Drees' for older people.

What does all this mean for the Dutch population? The income security of people aged between 18 and 64 years has fallen by 34% since 1980 (Figure 2). If we look at the entire adult population, however, this reduction shrinks to just 10%, as the positive development among pensioners partly cancels out the negative trend in the potential labour force.

The above makes no allowance for the fact that the majority of the population are not retired. In addition, everyone over retirement age receives the state pension, whereas most younger people do not live on benefit. If we take into account the population shares and benefit take-up, the picture reverses and we find that the income security of the population as a whole rose by 12% between 1980 and 2015. However, this improvement accrued exclusively to pensioners. I doubt whether this was Drees' original intention.

35 years of labour market security

But the decline in the income security of the labour force need not be such a problem as long as it is accompanied by an increase in labour market security. Let us therefore consider how working people have fared in the

Netherlands over the last 35 years.[14] I constructed an indicator for this as well. It is derived from two OECD series on the legal protection of people in permanent employment and of people with temporary contracts or working through a temporary work agency. The indicators relate to dismissal protection and severance pay, the number of times that a temporary contract can be renewed, and so on. The indicator covers a long period, but is more limited than the income protection measure.[15] I have assumed that the fairly stable picture at the start of the time series also applies for the period 1980-1984, for which there are no data.[16]

The trend in employee protection shows much less fluctuation than the trend for incomes. Until the middle of the 1990s, the protection for people with permanent employment contracts fell somewhat (Figure 3). The introduction of the Flexibility and Security Act (*Wet Flexibiliteit en Zekerheid*) in 1999 widened the gap slightly between people with temporary contracts and in temporary work agency employment on the one hand and employees with permanent contracts on the other. In 2009, the severance pay for people with permanent contracts and a long employment record was reduced by a limited amount, due to a change in the calculation formula applied by the regional courts. The Work and Security Act (*Wet Werk en Zekerheid - WWZ*) came into force last year; the net effect on the protection of permanent employees was estimated to be neutral. However, the new rules on the maximum number of contract renewals and their cumulative duration slightly improved the statutory protection of temporary employees, cancelling out roughly three-fifths of the small decline they had suffered under the Flexibility and Security Act. A few caveats need to be applied here, however. It is still too early to evaluate the impact of some aspects of the Work and Security Act, and the reactions of employers to the new law are also left out of consideration here. Those responses can vary between small and large companies or between different sectors.[17]

To measure total employment protection, the OECD adds together the two series; but that is not a good indicator of labour market security. Suppose a given country achieves maximum scores for permanent and temporary workers; in that case it is still likely that people without permanent contracts will be the first to lose their jobs.

Figure 3 Employee protection by contract type (1980-2015)

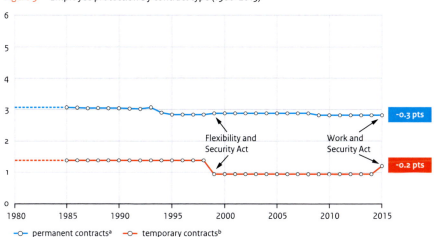

a Indicators of protection: Procedural inconveniences (notification procedures, delay to start a notice); notice period and level of severance pay for no-fault individual dismissals; difficulty of dismissal (definition of unfair dismissal; trial period; compensation; reinstatement).
b Indicators of protection: Admissibility of fixed term contracts and temporary work agency employment; restrictions on number of successive contracts/renewals; maximum cumulative duration of contracts/renewals.

Source: OECD Employment Protection Statistics (1985-2013); CPB (2014-2015)

Figure 4 Labour market security below the pension age (1980-2015; index scores, 1980=100)

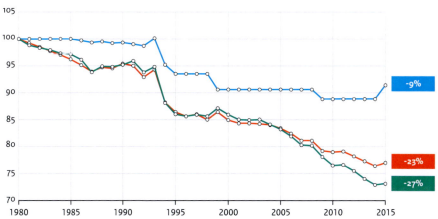

An analysis of the Dutch Labour Supply Panel supports this. If other conditions are the same, the odds ratio (whether or not people retain their job over a period of two years) is a factor of 0.34 lower for temporary workers than for people with permanent contracts. If we take this into account when adding together the scores, we find that the labour market security of all persons in waged employment declined by 9% between 1980 and 2015 (Figure 4).[18]

However, this calculation does not reflect the relative growth in the number of people in temporary employment.[19] If we weight the scores to take account of the changes in the shares of permanent and temporary wage-earners, we find that labour market security has fallen more sharply since 1980, by 23%.[20] This trend was interrupted in 2015 for the first time in years. But it is quite possible that the 'wwz effect' will not prove to be a turning point in the years ahead, but will merely create a small upward blip in a long-term downward trend.

For self-employed people, the certainty of work is by definition limited.[21] The third line in the figure shows that labour market security falls further if we include this group, declining by a total of 27% since 1980. This is mainly due to the sharp rise in the share of self-employed people over the last 12 years, especially sole traders.

This means that the decline in labour market security is almost as great as the reduction in income security that we saw earlier for people below the pension age. The diminishing income protection of the potential labour force is thus not offset by greater labour market security. On the contrary, over the past 35 years insecurity has increased in both respects, especially since the middle of the 1990s.[22]

Changed segmentation and citizens' discontent

Have the changes in income and labour market security affected the social position of Dutch citizens? And does the growth in 'taking part in uncertainty' help us understand why the tone of public reactions is much more shrill today than in the time of Willem Drees? Put differently, do the institutional changes we have just discussed work through into social segmentation and the way in which people view Dutch society? These are two eminently sociological questions. A definitive answer would require further research into the causal links and underlying processes. However, based on what is already known, we can derive a first impression.

To do this, I will draw on the scp study *Verschil in Nederland* ('Disparities in the Netherlands') from 2014. For this study, we carried out a representative survey of just under 3,000 adults, supplemented by administrative record data from Statistics Netherlands (cbs). Based on the resources to which people had access, the Dutch population falls into six groups (cf. Figure 5).[23] In part, this segmentation is connected to variation in economic capital: the amount of money people have, their occupation, their educational credentials and their skills. However, it is also linked to differences in:
- the social capital embedded in their networks;
- the cultural capital as reflected in their lifestyle, command of language and digital skills;
- and the three aspects of person capital: their physical condition, mental strength or weakness, and their attractiveness (physical, mental and aesthetic capital).

The study measured these aspects at just one point in time. Consequently, strictly speaking we cannot determine whether the six population segments are the result of changes in the income and labour market security I discussed earlier. However, for three of them this seems a rather plausible assumption. The *comfortable retirees* group are probably partly the product of the increased income protection for older persons. The *insecure workers* are mentally vulnerable and are on the periphery of the labour market; and it is difficult to see that as unconnected to the increased labour market insecurity. The *precariat* are often forced to rely on minimum benefits, which have deteriorated over time, or on a reduced state pension; the elderly persons within this group have not experienced the general improvement in old age pensions. In the precariat, the declining income security is probably reflected in the social segmentation. However, these people face other problems as well: they are also at the bottom of the ladder when it comes to person capital, social networks and cultural resources.

Figure 5   Segmentation of the Dutch population (2014)

six groups, ranked by total capital

established upper echelon

15% of the population

Most capital. Highest education level, highest incomes and assets. Overrepresentation of self-employed persons and retirees. Highest share of owner-occupied homes; most home equity. Most mental capital. Most luxurious lifestyle. Extensive social and instrumental networks.

High proportion in middle age (35-64 years); few young people (average age 52 years). Many cohabitees. Almost all Dutch natives (small number of Western migrants). Highest proportion of men. Many non-voters, many centre-right liberals (VVD) or social-liberals (D66). Average happiness score: 8.1 out of 10.

privileged younger people

13% of the population

Second highest education level. Low income and assets. Lots of rented homes; where owner-occupied, little home equity. Many students. Relatively large number of self-employed. Physically the healthiest, aesthetically the most attractive. Most digital skills and best command of English. Extensive social and reasonable instrumental networks.

Many young people; many single persons (average age 36). Relatively high proportion of non-Western migrants. Relatively high share of men. Lowest attendance at church, mosque or other place of worship. Often live in the urbanised west of the Netherlands. One third do not vote or don't know. Preference for social-liberals (D66). Happiness: 7.7.

employed middle echelon

27% of the population

Above-average economic capital. Highest labour participation rate, almost exclusively as waged employees. Often own their home, with limited home equity. Score for other three forms of capital at or just below average. Small instrumental network, reasonable social network.

Aged under 65; wide age spread (average 42 years). Many families with children. Few non-voters, but 20% don't know which party they support. Where they do know, mainly centre-right liberals (VVD) and social-liberals (D66), followed by socialist party (SP). Happiness: 7.6.

comfortable retirees	insecure workers	precariat

17% of the population	**14%** of the population	**15%** of the population
Generally low education level. Reasonable income, substantial assets; often home-owners; high home equity (negative equity rare). Lots of old age pension, but also early retirement pension/independent means. High perceived mental and aesthetic capital; less physical capital. Little cultural capital (poor command of English and deficient digital skills) Fairly luxurious lifestyle.	Average education level. Lots of incomes in the lowest decile. Focus on the labour market, but often in an uncertain position (temporary contracts, unemployment). Lowest liquid assets. High proportion of renters and when home-owners, often negative equity. Least mental capital. Reasonable command of English and digital skills. Reasonable social network, but smaller instrumental network.	**Least capital.** Lowest education level, most often on benefits or meagre pension. Often in rented housing and virtually no assets. Fairly high proportion of retirees. Physically most unhealthy and overweight. Least luxurious lifestyle; lowest digital skills and poorest command of English. Virtually no instrumental network; small social network.
Mostly aged 50 or over (average: 64 years). Relatively often attend church, mosque or other place of worship. Generally vote, mainly for Christian Democrats (CDA), followed by centre-right liberals (VVD) and social-liberals (D66). Relatively high proportion of over-50 voters. Happiness: 7.6.	Middle-aged (35-64 years) and below (25-34 years); few over-65s (average age 41 years). Relatively high proportion of migrants. Highest share of women. Relatively high proportion of lone-parent families. Largest share of non-voters. Also many supporters of socialist party (SP), right-wing populist party (PVV) and social-liberals (D66). Happiness: 6.1.	Average age 62 years; few young people, but wide age spread. Many single elderly persons. Highest attendance at church, mosque or other place of worship. Relatively high share of migrants and women. Many non-voters and don't-know's. Voters often support socialist party (SP), right-wing populist party (PVV) or Labour Party (PvdA). Happiness: 6.3.

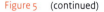

Figure 5   (continued)

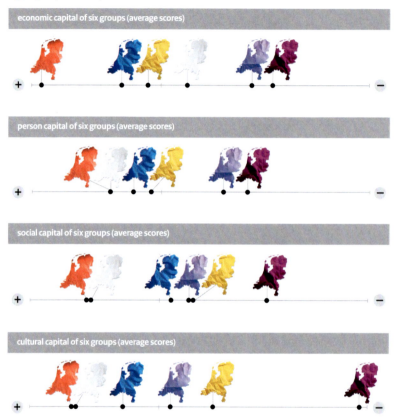

Source: C. Vrooman, M. Gijsberts & J. Boelhouwer (ed.) (2014). *Verschil in Nederland - Sociaal en Cultureel Rapport 2014*. Den Haag: Sociaal en Cultureel Planbureau (pp. 314-315).

Three other groups have probably been less affected by the growing trend towards 'taking part in uncertainty'. Members of the *established upper echelon* and *privileged younger people* have access to plentiful resources and are often able to manage on their own. This also holds for the *employed middle echelon*, mostly comprising couples (usually with children) in which one partner works full-time and the other part-time. At least, this applies to them as long as they are able to keep their jobs and maintain their good health. It may be that for some members of the employed middle echelon the increased income and labour market insecurity has given rise to concerns about their own and their children's future.

The indignant emails received by today's government ministers can be seen as an expression of citizens' discontent. The writers of those letters are dissatisfied with the way the Netherlands is going, and hold politicians responsible for this. The same SCP survey contains a great deal of information on this. I have combined that information into a single indicator.[24] It is based on survey questions on the following topics:[25]
– The perceived deficiency of social protection;
– Aversion to cultural differences;
– Rejection of ever closer European integration;
– A sense of political abandonment;
– And the perceived failure of the Dutch elite.

Figure 6 presents the average scores for citizens' discontent according to the classification used in 'Disparities in the Netherlands'. For the insecure workers and precariat segments it proved useful to distinguish between the discontent of Dutch natives and non-Western migrants. This leaves us with eight population groups.[26] A higher score means that people think that:
– the government should be doing more to counter economic inequalities;
– the differences in the norms, values and religion of Dutch natives and migrants are problematic, and migrants should adapt to the Dutch culture;
– European integration has gone too far;
– the government does too little for ordinary people; people have no influence over government policy; and ministers and MPs pay no heed to what people think;
– the elite put their own interests first; they have not done anything to earn their position in society; they don't understand ordinary people; and they are responsible for the fact that things in the Netherlands are moving in the wrong direction.

The figure shows that there is little discontent in the established upper echelon or among privileged younger people, and it is also below average in the employed middle echelon. The comfortable retirees come just above the average. By contrast, discontent is high to very high among the insecure workers and the precariat. At least, this is the case for Dutch natives; the discontent among non-Western migrants is much lower. These differences cannot be traced back to the individual components of the discontent, nor to the divergent education levels of the population groups. [27]

About 23% of Dutch citizens score above a threshold value indicating a high level of discontent. [28] The small pie charts in the figure show how this high discontent is divided over the eight population groups. Non-Western migrants in the insecure workers and precariat groups account for a negligible share of the discontent (1-3%). The established upper echelon and privileged younger people are also clearly underrepresented. Three-quarters of discontented citizens are natives who fall into the insecure workers and precariat groups, comfortable retirees and members of the employed middle echelon. Discontent is below average in this last category; but because the employed middle echelon is much larger than the other social segments, the number of discontented people turns out fairly high.

Citizens' discontent is thus concentrated in those groups that have been confronted with declining protection, and especially the Dutch natives among them. It is also widespread among those who may fear that their own or their children's security could be jeopardised in the future. I would therefore advance the proposition that the indignant emails received by members of cabinet today are sent mainly by discontented Dutch natives belonging to the insecure workers or precariat groups, as well as by sections of the comfortable retirees and employed middle echelon. A divergence in the digital skills and time constraints of the population segments could lead to some distortion in the distribution of senders. These emails nonetheless reflect the widespread discontent among more than a fifth of the adult Dutch population.

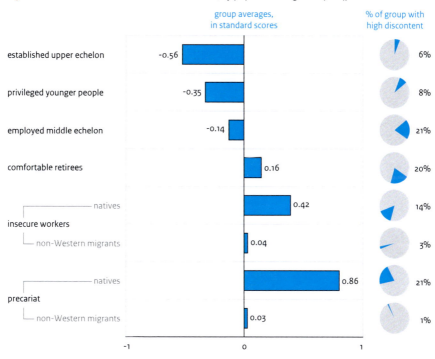

Figure 6   Citizens' discontent in the Netherlands, by population segment (2014)

Source: scp, Survey Verschil in Nederland 2014

The contrast with the grateful public reactions sent to Willem Drees thus appears to be partly connected to institutional reforms. Of course, labour market and income insecurity were much higher during Drees' time than today. People like Mr Van Hooff and Sister Jenkens were lifted from their misery by Drees' policy, and this gave rise to the idea that the government would begin looking after all citizens better. Until 1980, the expansion of the Dutch welfare state meant this expectation was met. After 35 years of changes in the social security system and the labour market, the situation today is different. Many people have experienced the growing insecurity personally in recent years; others may believe the protection they currently still have is under threat, and fear that they will be unable to provide that protection for themselves in the future. It is likely that the growing 'taking part in uncertainty' has impacted on the social fabric of the Netherlands. It has probably also fuelled the discontent among people with few resources and those who fear a decline in their circumstances.

I hope to make the relationships between changes in regulations, social segmentation and social cohesion one of the central topics for my Chair. This appears to fit in very well with this University's strategic theme of 'Institutions for Open Societies'.

The importance of networks

However, my work will begin with a study of the relationship between people's social networks and benefit dependency.[29] Figure 7 gives an impression of how important this topic is. The SCP survey reveals that there are a number of differences between the networks of people with jobs and those in receipt of unemployment or social assistance benefit.[30] Country of origin plays a distinctive role here.[31]

At the top of the graph we see that those in work (indicated by the red line) have a much larger instrumental network than recipients of unemployment or social assistance benefit. This means that people with jobs know more influential persons who can help them advance in their lives.[32] The instrumental networks of native and non-Western benefit recipients (the orange and blue areas) are small. Almost two-thirds of Dutch natives in receipt of unemployment or social assistance benefit do not know any influential people at all, and the figure is even higher – almost three-quarters – for their non-Western migrant counterparts. The limited instrumental networks of benefit recipients can pose an obstacle to finding work.
Working people are also surrounded by more people who can help them in their day-to-day lives when needed (on the left in the figure). Dutch native benefit recipients have a smaller support network, but their disadvantage is less than for instrumental relationships. Once again, non-Western migrants in receipt of benefit lag a long way behind.

Figure 7   Networks of benefit recipients and (self-)employed (2014)

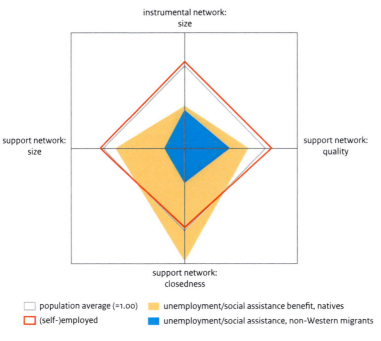

Source: SCP, Survey Verschil in Nederland 2014

In addition, the support networks of (self-)employed people are of higher quality: they are more often able to discuss personal issues with others. The gap between Dutch natives and migrants in receipt of benefits is less pronounced on this aspect (on the right of the figure).

The pattern is different when it comes to the closeness of the support network (shown at the bottom of the figure). In 63% of cases, the members of the networks with which Dutch native unemployment or social assistance benefit recipients have intensive contact (almost) all know each other. That is a higher proportion than for those in work. In other words, the support networks of native benefit recipients are smaller and of poorer quality than those of workers, but are more close-knit. This may make it easier to mobilise support because of the good mutual contacts. However, it is doubtful whether this close-knit group will be able to deploy many resources.

Moreover, those resources may easily become diluted, as it is likely that several members of the network will experience similar problems. On the other hand, the picture is more positive than for migrants on benefit, where members of the potential support networks often do not know each other.

A few caveats need to be applied to these findings. The measurement of network characteristics in the survey used was limited. People on disability benefit turn out to differ less from those in work than the unemployed and social assistance recipients (not shown in figure). We do not know whether the intriguing pattern in the graph corresponds with variations in job application behaviour and success. And if this does occur, the causal mechanism needs to be ascertained: is it mainly the information embedded in the networks that drives effective behaviour, or rather the prevailing social norms? Or does the causal connection operate the other way round, with benefit dependency generating different networks, for example because, the longer they remain out of work, the more the circle in which people move shrinks to include only people like themselves? Finally, earlier research suggests that there are wide differences between people of Turkish or Chinese origin, for example, and between the first and later generations of migrants.[33] No allowance was made for that diversity here.

The results do however suggest that the project 'From network to work?' (*Van netwerk naar werk?*), which addresses these kinds of questions, offers promise both for science and policy. If network characteristics influence the likelihood of benefit dependency, it may be useful to put unemployed people and benefit recipients in contact with 'people from the outside'. This will enable them to increase the amount of information within their networks and may help to break through social expectations or a negative spiral. I think that Marcus Kristiansen and Sanne Boschman will shed light on this over the coming years in the project that is linked to this Chair. Under the supervision of Ineke Maas and myself, they will be performing interesting and important research.

Acknowledgements

I am drawing to a close, and would like to take this opportunity to thank a number of people and organisations. First, the Executive Board and the Faculty of Social and Behavioural Sciences at Utrecht University for the confidence they have placed in me. Tanja van der Lippe and Werner Raub have put a great deal of effort into embedding the Chair solidly within the Faculty, and the colleagues and secretariat of the Sociology Department have made sure that I have quickly felt at home here over the last few months.

A great debt of thanks is owed to Instituut Gak, which has endowed this Chair and which has been generous enough to fund positions for a doctoral and postdoctoral researcher. In particular, Bert de Jong and Boudien Krol have done excellent work in ensuring the success of this initiative. Without their vision and persistence, it would not have happened.

I would also like to thank the Director of the Netherlands Institute for Social Research|SCP, Kim Putters, and his predecessor, Paul Schnabel. They have both made considerable efforts to establish this connection between SCP and the University, and supported me throughout the process.

Finally, I would like to thank my inspiring PhD supervisors, Wil Arts and Jaap Dronkers. I have learned much from them. Sadly, just today I have heard that Jaap has been rushed into hospital. I send him and his family my very best wishes.

All that now remains is for me to return to the intriguing experience that I mentioned at the start of my discourse. This inaugural lecture is linked in a special way to my deceased parents, Nelly Hilberding and Kees Vrooman. They stood at the beginning of the journey that has ultimately carried me here today, and I am very grateful to them for that. But there is a further connection. Before describing it I should say that I did not have a religious upbringing, and that metaphysical questions have never interested me greatly, not even as I have grown older.

Some years ago, when I was about to obtain my doctorate, I spoke to the Beadle of Tilburg University to set a date for the ceremony. We agreed on 4 September, a few months later. I wanted to get the process done with as quickly as possible, so simply chose the first available moment, though I was also dimly aware that there was something significant about that date. It was only later, sitting in the train on the way home, that I realised that my father had died on 4 September. Well, I thought, that's actually quite nice – in a sense he will be present, and that sad date will acquire a more complex significance in the future.

Then last year I was talking with the Beadle of Utrecht University to arrange a date for my inaugural lecture. She suggested today, 30 March 2016, with an alternative date much further in the future. Once again I thought, I'll take the first possible moment; this is not something that should be put off. But yet again I was possessed of a strange feeling. This time, the realisation took only five minutes to penetrate my consciousness: 30 March is the date of my mother's death...

The probability of such a coincidence occurring twice is roughly 100 times as great as the probability of winning first prize in the New Year lottery.

But that is still highly unlikely. This repeated chance occurrence means that as I stand here today, I experience a strong connection with my parents. I even feel something – contrary to my *habitus* – akin to a sense of predetermination.

The link with what went before, but ended too soon, makes this an especially important day for me. I therefore dedicate this lecture to my deceased parents, and thank you for being present to hear it.

Dixi.

Notes

1 Stichting Willem Dreeslezing, *Vader der ouden van dagen – brieven aan Willem Drees* (Den Haag 1998: Uitgeverij De Nieuwe Haagsche, pp. 26, 31, 48); J. Gaemers (ed.), *Vier stoelen in de hemel – Brieven aan Drees over de ouderdomsvoorziening* (Den Haag 2008: Ando/Stichting Willem Dreeslezing). This work also describes how, in April 1947, Drees was hailed by the senior citizens' association as the 'Father of the Elderly', an honour he accepted when a delegation from the association visited the Ministry of Social Affairs. The delegates presented Drees with a fountain pen which they hoped "he would be able to use to sign many more pieces of social legislation".

2 See, for instance, the political clamour over the *Teeven Deal*: www.reuters.com/article/us-dutch-politics-resignations-idUSKBN0M52AM20150309; www.reuters.com/article/us-dutch-politics-id USKBN0TZ23P20151216.

3 The co-resident rule stipulates that the level of minimum income benefits is reduced when recipients share their dwelling with adult persons, irrespective of the nature of their relationship. The higher the number of co-residing adults, the lower the benefit level.

4 www.facebook.com/LodewijkAsscher/posts/947091382045589.

5 In fact social security was already a contested issue in its post-war period of expansion. It took ten years to convert the *Noodwet Ouderdomsvoorziening* into a national insurance-based system, in the form of the General Old Age Pensions Act (AOW); and the introduction of the Social Assistance Act (*Algemene Bijstandswet*) in 1965 and the Invalidity Insurance Act (*Wet op de Arbeidsongeschiktheidsverzekering*) in 1967 was also preceded by years of heated Parliamentary and public debate. See G.M.J. Veldkamp (with B. le Blanc and A. Bosscher), *Inleiding tot de sociale zekerheid en de toepassing ervan in Nederland en België* (Deventer 1978-1980, 2 vols); J.M. Roebroek & M. Hertogh, *'De beschavende invloed des tijds'; Twee eeuwen sociale politiek, verzorgingsstaat en sociale zekerheid in Nederland* (Den Haag 1998: Cosz/Vuga).

6 J. de Hart & P. van Houwelingen, 'De eenzame elite' in: C. Vrooman, M. Gijsberts & J. Boelhouwer (eds.). *Verschil in Nederland - Sociaal en Cultureel Rapport 2014* (Den Haag 2014: Sociaal en Cultureel Planbureau, pp. 203-224).

7 The oldest known occurrence of the term 'social security' is in a speech given by Simón Bolívar in 1819 to mark the independence of Venezuela, in which he argued that: "The most perfect system of government is one which produces the most happiness, the most *social security* and the most political stability". However, the concept only gained currency following the introduction of the Social Security Act in the US in 1935. The concept was not yet defined at this time: it referred to the economic security provided to the community (society) via the law. The International Labour Organisation went a step further in the 1940s:

"As the State is an association of citizens which exists for the sake of their general well-being, it is a proper function of the State to promote social security. [... It comprises] such schemes as provide the citizen with benefits designed to prevent or cure disease, to support him when unable to earn and to restore him to gainful activity. Not all such measures, however, can be considered as affording security. [...] Security is a state of mind as well as an objective fact. To enjoy security, one must have confidence that the benefits will be available when required, and, in order to afford security, the protection must be adequate in quality and quantity."

The ILO expanded on this theme in Convention no. 102, published in 1952, which defined the chief social security risks to be covered. This is characteristic of the 'narrow' definition of social security, in which its main purpose is income protection. It provides a guaranteed minimum income or guarantees – to a degree – to maintain the acquired standard of living. The instruments deployed to achieve this consist of legally mandated social insurance arrangements (such as retirement pension for employees) and national provisions such as social assistance benefits. Based on these arrangements, benefits and resources in kind are offered when clearly defined risks manifest themselves (old age, death of a breadwinner, unemployment, incapacity for work, etc.). The narrow definition of social security is in fairly common use, but has the disadvantage that it is equated to formal income arrangements which target specific and traditional risks; it does not include measures to mitigate the financial and social consequences of divorce, for example.

In the 'broad' definition, social security is theoretically concerned not just with income protection, but with ensuring security of work, health and participation in society. It involves the deployment not just of statutory government arrangements, but also includes what Berghman described as 'invisible social security'. Building on the work of Titmuss, he was referring to tax cuts and tax relief, payments and insurance linked to employment, and savings and insurance schemes that people arrange themselves (fiscal, occupational and private provisions). In the broad approach, the interventions do not consist solely of partial compensation for a falling or insufficient income; in principle, prevention and recovery should be given priority. Social security is also not focused exclusively on the traditional risks in the broad definition, but includes all forms of 'human damage', for example covering ecological decline or losses which only manifest themselves after many years. The disadvantage of the broad approach is that there is a danger of making social security all-embracing: the entire welfare state falls within this definition, plus all possible provisions that might be taken outside of the public sector. The broad definition is also a-sociological, with scant attention for behaviour, for the context in which the rules are established and applied, such as the interests and values that are at stake, or for the implications of the arrangements for society as a whole.

Elsewhere I have called for an institutional demarcation of social security, which is then understood as the *collectively defined rights, duties, conditions and potential sanctions which aim to generate positive social outcomes by protecting individual actors against economic deficits*. In this interpretation, social security is a collection of rules that are constructed within a community – institutions, in other words. Those rules relate to deficits of individuals that can be given an economic value: insufficient income, loss of work, the costs of medical provisions or social participation. They may be both formal and informal, may include laws or rules, or social norms and conventions. Rights and obligations are assigned in order to serve a higher purpose. There is an expectation that the rules will influence actors' behaviour, generating net positive results for the community. For example, people are forced to pay tax and espouse solidarity with others, so that the nation's wealth is shared more equitably; or people are given the opportunity to apply for benefit to prevent large numbers falling into poverty, potentially giving rise to social tensions. According to this institutional definition, social security embraces more than the traditional social insurance schemes and national provisions. On the other hand, it is not so all-embracing that the concept can no longer be analytically separated from the welfare state.

See: S. Bolívar, 'Discurso ante el congreso de Angustora, 15 de Febrero de 1819'. In: E. Mondolfi (ed.) *Bolívar: Ídeas de un espíritu visionario (Antología)* (Caracas (no date): Biblioteco del Pensamiento Venezolano); ILO, *Approaches to social security; An international survey* (Montreal 1944: International Labour Office, p. 80); R.M. Titmuss, 'The social division of welfare', in R.M. Titmuss, *Essays on the welfare state* (London 1958: Unwin University Books); J. Berghman, *De onzichtbare sociale zekerheid* (Deventer 1986: Kluwer); J.C. Vrooman, *Rules of Relief; Institutions of social security, and their impact.* (The Hague 2009: The Netherlands Institute for Social Research|SCP, pp. 111-208).

8   Initially the focus on participation in the Netherlands mainly related to the extension of active labour market policy ('work before income'). In recent years, however, increasing attention has been devoted to 'social participation'. This is a complex concept, which can refer to an additional policy objective, namely combating social exclusion. In other cases it refers to an alternative approach: informal delivery, in which citizens themselves provide for their own security, for example through savings or a membership of a 'bread fund' (*broodfonds*). There is also a third option, in which 'taking part' refers to the process of institutional decision-making, by involving client councils, bringing recipients and contributors on to the boards of pension funds, or through modern forms of civic involvement. In a final alternative, social participation is embedded in the rules, whereby people have to exhibit the 'right' behaviour in order to receive or be eligible for benefits or help. The recent requirement to do something in return for receiving Dutch social assistance benefits is an example of this approach.

9   R. Chandler, *The Long Good-Bye* (London 1953: Hamish Hamilton); B. Palier (ed.), *A Long Goodbye to Bismarck? The Politics of Welfare Reform in Continental Europe* (Amsterdam 2010: Amsterdam University Press). Drees was in fact critical of the way in which his successors expanded the welfare state, and probably would have favoured a more frugal system and an active integration policy.

10   For a more detailed description of these developments, see C. Vrooman 'Een succesvolle gedaantewisseling? De hervorming van de sociale zekerheid, 1985-2010', in *Tijdschrift voor Arbeidsvraagstukken* (2010: 4, pp. 358-377). This article is partly an update of the chapter on social security that I wrote for the Social and Cultural Report 1998 (*Sociaal en Cultureel Rapport 1998*). Also see e.g. J. van Gerwen & M.H.D. van Leeuwen (eds.), *Zoeken naar zekerheid – Risico's, preventie, verzekeringen en andere zekerheidsregelingen in Nederland 1500-2000; Deel 4: De welvaartsstaat* (Den Haag/Amsterdam 2000: Verbond van Verzekeraars/NEHA); M. van Gerven, *The broad tracks of path dependent benefit reform; A longitudinal study of social benefit reforms in three European countries, 1980–2006* (Helsinki 2008: Kela, Research Department); J. de Koning, 'Vorm boven inhoud: het actief arbeidsmarktbeleid in de afgelopen dertig jaar', in *Tijdschrift voor Arbeidsvraagstukken* (2010: 4, pp. 380-396); N. van Gestel, E. Vossen, S. Oomens & D. Hollanders, *Toekomst van de sociale zekerheid; Over preventie, provisie en participatie* (Den Haag 2013: Boom Lemma); F. de Kam, *Het land van beloften: Opbouw, crisis en toekomst van de verzorgingsstaat* (Amsterdam 2015: Atlas Contact); Nationaal Archief, *Een samenleving in beweging; Nederland tussen 1976 en 2005 in 200 trends en 100 hotspots* (Den Haag 2016: Nationaal Archief, pp. 203-208 and 291-372).

11   In the article in *Tijdschrift voor Arbeidsvraagstukken* cited earlier, I showed that the Dutch social security system changed between 1985 and 2010 from a hybrid form of the corporatist and social-democratic regime types towards the Scandinavian and Anglo-Saxon models (it became both more 'Swedish' and more 'American'). The analysis performed here includes more institutional

characteristics, covers a longer period – including all intervening years – and applies a different method.

Unlike with citizens' discontent, which is dealt with later, I opted not to use a scaling method to construct the measures for income and employee protection. The reason is that there is no underlying latent variable here that could be reflected in the indicators; rather, the indicators are building blocks for constructing a compound measure. Babbie refers in this regard to indicators as the 'cause' and 'effect' of the measure. In the former case, the indicators can be logically opposed or empirically weakly correlated, but are still valid elements for the compound measure. This occurs here, for example, with the indicators concerning the duration of the right to sick leave benefit and the period that an employer is required to continue paying a sick employee's salary. Both are necessary in order to obtain a good picture of the changing income protection of sick employees. However, the correlation is logically negative (r= -0.91). See chapter 6 in E.R. Babbie, *The Practice of Social Research* (Boston 2016: Cengage Learning).

12 Appendix 1 lists the indicators used. For each indicator, the original categories were ranked on a scale from 1 to 10, based on their theoretical minimum and maximum scores. If the indicator is not theoretically capped, its maximum level is set at the highest empirical value reached between 1980 and 2015. The indicators for each individual aspect (coverage, benefit conditions, benefit levels, maximum duration and reintegration) were weighted and added together; the weighting factors are also listed in Appendix 1. The scores on each aspect were subsequently combined (with equal weight) to produce a total score for each type of benefit scheme (state minimum pension, supplementary occupational pension, early retirement/pre-pension, surviving dependants' pension, unemployment insurance benefit, social assistance benefit, sick leave benefit and disability benefit). Finally, the applicable scores were added together to produce two compound measures of income protection above and below the retirement age. Appendix 2 shows the development of the scores for each specific type of benefit scheme over time.

13 This is exacerbated by the reducing weight of notional insured years. When the state old-age pension was introduced, it was decided that the years before 1957 would count in all cases, even if the person concerned was not a resident of the Netherlands at that time. This favourable condition no longer applies for the cohorts that started receiving state pension after 2007.

14 The OECD recently also developed a measure for labour market security. The Netherlands does well on that criteron, coming fourth in a group of 34 countries. However, this criterion is not available for a long period, and moreover mixes labour and income security. Analytically, it is better to keep these two separate, because developments do not necessarily go in the same direction. A. Hijzen & B. Menyhert, *Measuring labour market security and assessing its implications for individual well-being* (Paris 2016: Organisation for Economic Co-operation and Development) (http://dx.doi.org/10.1787/5jm58qvzd6s4-en).

15 Version 1 of the OECD criterion was used here. This comprises eight indicators for permanent contracts and six for temporary employment and work agency employment. The protection in the event of collective dismissal is left out of consideration here, but according to version 3 of the criterion, this did not change in the Netherlands between 1997 and 2013. See D. Venn, *Legislation, collective bargaining and enforcement: Updating the OECD employment protection indicators* (Paris 2009: Organisation for Economic Co-operation and Development). The data are taken from http://www.oecd.org/employment/emp/oecdindicatorsofemploymentprotection.htm and were

supplemented for 2014 and 2015 from a publication by the Netherlands Bureau for Economic Policy Analysis (CPB): *Gevolgen Wet Werk en Zekerheid voor werkgelegenheid* (Den Haag 2013: Centraal Planbureau, pp. 6-7).

16 By international standards, total employee protection in the Netherlands is just above the average. The Netherlands scores especially well for the protection of permanent employees; in 2008 only Germany, the Czech Republic, Portugal, Sweden and Slovenia ranked higher. The comparatively high Dutch protection score for people with permanent jobs is due to the rules on severance pay and procedural obstacles to dismissal; the notice period for individual dismissal is relatively short. The Netherlands scores around the average for the protection of work agency employment, but the protection of temporary workers is limited compared with other countries. See also C. Vrooman, E. Josten & J.D. Vlasblom, 'Minder ontslagbescherming, meer werkende ouderen?', in: SCP, *Startklaar voor vier jaar; een verkenning van publieke prestaties voor de kabinetsformatie 2012.* (Den Haag 2012: Sociaal en Cultureel Planbureau, pp. 81-97).

17 On balance, the introduction of the WWZ did not lead to any changes in the protection of permanent employees on the OECD indicator: protection increased for dismissal judgments through the Employee Insurance Agency (UWV) route, while it declined in the trajectory through the regional courts. The protection of temporary and work agency employment rises by 0.2 points because of the changes in the rule on consecutive contracts. People working through employment agencies have to work for 5.5 years before being entitled to a permanent contract, much longer than 'normal' temporary employees. This is due to the collective labour agreement provisions on employment agencies, which stipulate that the first 78 weeks are discounted for the right to a permanent appointment (*uitzendbeding*, or 'work agency proviso'); and on the number and maximum duration of temporary contracts once that criterion no longer applies (six contracts in four years). Compared with the situation before the introduction of the WWZ, when the work agency proviso lasted indefinitely, this theoretically offers slightly more protection. Two other legal elements introduced in the WWZ, the abolition of a probationary period for temporary contracts and equal treatment of payroll employees, have no influence on the scores, because the chosen indicators are not sensitive to these policy changes. The version of the OECD indicators used here contains no indicators for collective dismissal protection. However, since the first available measurement year (1997), these have remained virtually stable in the Netherlands, and were not changed in the WWZ.

18 Babbie (op. cit.) points out that when constructing compound measures, the components should in principle be added together with equal weights, unless there is a convincing reason not to do so. In the income security criterion discussed earlier, there is no need to do this when adding together the protection of the potential labour force and pensioners, because the components are theoretically the same (level, duration, coverage and conditions); some individual indicators are even identical for both age groups, using the same scale (e.g. the amount of the guaranteed minimum income). As regards labour market security, the components in the criteria for permanent and temporary employees are by contrast very different, and there are no items that are shared between the two. Consequently, while in these two cases we measure the relevant statutory protection, it is not valid to simply add together the protection scores for permanent and temporary employees in order to produce an overall labour market security measure. If permanent and temporary employees both attain the maximum protection score of six on their

specific indicators, the labour market position of the latter can still be more insecure. To allow for this, a probit model was estimated using the data from the scp Labour Supply Panel 2000-2014. The dependent variable is the probability that employees will keep their jobs, given their type of contract two years previously (permanent/temporary), taking account of the effects of full-time or part-time work. The model, which was developed by Dr J.D. Vlasblom, also corrects for the influence of age, sex, education level, economic situation (indicated by measurement year), marital status, presence of children aged 12 or under, and subjective evaluation of health.

19   According to the OECD, out of the dependent labour force only one in 12 people in the Netherlands were not in permanent jobs in 1985 (7.6%); in 2014 this had risen to more than one in five (21.7%). The figure for 2015 was estimated on the basis of a regression analysis. Source: OECD, *Temporary employment (indicator)*, doi: 10.1787/75589b8a-en (accessed on 4 February 2016).

20   It is however striking that the effect of the introduction of the Flexibility and Security Act in 1999 is positive after applying weighting. This is because the declining protection of temporary employees resulting from the Act was accompanied by a slight improvement in the protection of workers on permanent contracts (see Figure 3), and the latter group carries more weight. Moreover, 1999 was one of the few years when the share of people with permanent employment contracts increased slightly (from 87.2% to 88.0% in the OECD series used here).

21   The work security of self-employed people depends on how successfully they are able to win long-term contracts, and on the willingness of consumers and businesses to buy their goods or services. The Netherlands Civil Code distinguishes between an *overeenkomst van aanneming* ('contracting agreement'), which relates to the performance of physical activities, such as building a house; an *overeenkomst van opdracht* ('services agreement') which covers the performance of non-physical activities, e.g. provided by a freelancer; and other agreements (e.g. franchise, distribution, collaboration). In principle, none of these contract forms constitutes an employment relationship under Dutch law, which implies there is no legal employee protection. However, if the contract is terminated early – and there is no question of breach, non-performance or nullity – there may be a right to (partial) payment of the contracted sum, or of compensation. If the case is legally tested in the courts, it may also transpire in retrospect that an employment relationship did exist, and in that case the employee protection applies with retroactive force. In addition, working conditions legislation does afford self-employed workers some protection: those who commission their services are responsible for providing good working conditions, and can be held liable for accidents that occur during the performance of the activities. Self-employed workers also enjoy income protection through social security contribution exemptions, the general self-employed person's tax deduction, and specific tax deductions for business expenses, for the depreciation of equipment and business assets, for pension contributions and for certain investments. There are also specific forms of such 'fiscal social security' for start-ups and SMEs.

22   Self-employed workers are actually a highly diverse group. Some are perfectly capable of dealing with this insecurity and would not want anything to change. Others experienced for themselves during the recent recession how unprotected their work is when the economy is not going well. See e.g. E. Josten, J.D. Vlasblom & C. Vrooman, *Bevrijd of beklemd? Werk, inhuur, inkomen en welbevinden van zzp'ers* (Den Haag 2014: Sociaal en Cultureel Planbureau).

23 The six groups were identified through a latent class analysis of the following indicators.

Economic capital:
- educational attainment level (primary; lower secondary; higher secondary; tertiary);
- labour market position (unemployed; (early) retirement; otherwise inactive; student; waged employment; self-employed) ;
- standardised disposable income (decile 1; 2-3; 4-5; 6-9; percentile 90-99; percentile 100);
- liquid assets (negative; €0-5k; €5-50k; €50-500k; > €500k);
- housing assets (negative; renter; positive first tertile; second tertile; third tertile).

Social capital:
- social support, quantity (frequency of contacts with family, friends, neighbours);
- social support, quality (number of people with whom one can discuss personal matters);
- instrumental support (number of personal acquaintances in influential occupations).

Cultural capital:
- life style (holidays abroad; eating in expensive restaurants; attending classical music concerts and theatre, visiting art galleries/museums);
- digital skills (ability to use a word processor; to install computer software; to arrange PC security);
- command of the English language (none; limited; fair; good; native speaker).

Person capital:
- physical (subjective health evaluation; difficulty climbing stairs);
- mental (self-confidence; negative self-image; suffered from depression for at least two weeks in the past year);
- aesthetic (questionnaire items 'The way I look is just fine' and 'Most people think I look attractive'; 10-point scale);
- body mass index (serious overweight; overweight; underweight; normal weight).

Cf. J. Boelhouwer, M. Gijsberts & C. Vrooman, 'Nederland in meervoud', in: C. Vrooman, M. Gijsberts & J. Boelhouwer (eds.). *Verschil in Nederland - Sociaal en Cultureel Rapport 2014* (Den Haag 2014: Sociaal en Cultureel Planbureau, pp. 281-320).

24 Dekker and Den Ridder used five items from the same survey to construct an indicator for political dissatisfaction. However, this measure covers fewer topics and is not linked by the authors to the typology of the six population groups. See P. Dekker & J. den Ridder, 'Het politiek-culturele verschil', in: C. Vrooman, M. Gijsberts & J. Boelhouwer (eds.). *Verschil in Nederland - Sociaal en Cultureel Rapport 2014* (Den Haag 2014: Sociaal en Cultureel Planbureau, pp. 187-189).

25 Most aspects were measured on separate scales, which were constructed using nonlinear principal component analysis. The scaling of all variables was based on a spline ordinal measurement level. The category 'don't know' and nonresponse items were imputed with the quantifications of the modal response category. Each scale comprises the object scores on the first component, with average 0 and standard deviation 1.

The scale for the *perceived deficiency of social protection* (alpha=0.75) contains the responses to the following survey questions (recoded in the same direction):

a. 'The solidarity between young and old is under pressure'; strongly disagree (1) → strongly agree (10);

b. Preference for more self/government responsibility: 'People should take more responsibility for looking after themselves' (1) → 'The government should take more responsibility for ensuring that everyone receives what they need' (10);

c. Aversion to income inequality: 'Differences in income should be wider' (1) → 'Differences in income should be smaller' (10);

d. Aversion to wealth inequality: 'Differences in wealth should be wider' (1) → 'Differences in wealth should be smaller' (10).

The scale for *aversion to cultural differences* (alpha=0.80) is based on the following survey questions:

e. 'Differences in norms and values between natives and non-natives are a problem'; strongly disagree (1) → strongly agree (10);

f. 'Differences in religion between natives and non-natives are a problem'; strongly disagree (1) → strongly agree (10);

g. Migrants living in the Netherlands should be able to retain their own culture, or should adapt: 'Retain own culture' (1) → 'Adapt fully' (10).

The scale for *political abandonment* (alpha=0.72) is based on the following survey questions:

h. 'The government doesn't do enough for people like me'; strongly disagree (1) → strongly agree (5);

i. 'People like me have no influence at all over what the government does'; strongly disagree (1) → strongly agree (5);

j. 'MPs and government ministers don't care very much what people like me think'; strongly disagree (1) → strongly agree (5).

The scale for the *perceived failure of the Dutch elite* (alpha=0.74) is based on the following survey questions (recoded in the same direction):

k. 'How much trust do you have in Parliament at the moment?'; complete trust (1) → no trust at all (10);

l. 'The elite don't understand anything about me'; completely disagree (1) → completely agree (10);

m. 'The elite mainly look after their own interests'; completely disagree (1) → completely agree (10);

n. 'People who belong to the elite have usually earned their special position'; completely agree (1) → completely disagree (10);

o. Contribution of the elite to national development: 'Thanks to the elite, the Netherlands is going in the right direction' (1) → 'Thanks to the elite, the Netherlands is going in the wrong direction' (10).

The *rejection of further European integration* was measured using one survey question, the responses to which were expressed using standard scores:

p. Agreement with or rejection of further European integration: 'European integration needs to go further' (1) →'European integration has already gone too far' (10).

Factor analysis indicated that the individual scales and the separate 'European' item can be traced back to a single underlying dimension; from the second factor onwards, the eigenvalue is less than 1. The compound scale for citizens' discontent was constructed by tallying up the scores on the five components and standardising the summary measure thus obtained. The reliability of the scale is good (alpha=0.73), and cannot be improved by leaving out any one of the components.

A separate factor analysis was used to investigate whether citizens' discontent is also related to the *Schwartz Human Values*, on which the scp survey included a number of questions (S.H. Schwartz, 'An overview of the Schwartz theory of basic values', in *Psychology and Culture* (2012:1; http://dx.doi.org/10.9707/2307-0919.1116)). This was found not to be the case. The values universalism, tradition, power, achievement and hedonism do show some correlation with the six population groups (see Boelhouwer, Gijsberts &Vrooman, op. cit., pp. 303-304), but in the additional factor analysis these items end up on different dimensions, separate from the discontent as measured here.

26　The established upper echelon and comfortable retirees groups contain virtually no non-Western migrants, so there is little point in making a distinction by ethnic origin. By contrast, the privileged younger people and employed middle echelon do contain non-Western migrants. The level of discontent in both these groups is slightly greater among non-Western migrants than among Dutch natives. It is by far the lowest among Western migrants; these probably consist in part of expats and knowledge workers with a cosmopolitan outlook.

27　The difference between Dutch natives and non-Western migrants at the bottom of the ladder recurs in virtually all forms of discontent on which the scale is based. The only exception is 'failure of the elite' in the insecure workers group, where migrants score higher than natives. The contrast in discontent therefore cannot be explained by a lower resistance to cultural differences among non-Western migrants. However, the outcomes do not imply that there is no discontent among migrants; but their discontent is focused on aspects that were not included in the indicator, such as discrimination on the labour market, lack of recognition of their own norms and values, and Dutch traditions that are perceived as insulting or racist, such as *Sinterklaas'* assistant 'Black Pete' (see J. Dagevos & W, Huijnk, 'Segmentatie langs etnische grenzen' in: C. Vrooman, M. Gijsberts & J. Boelhouwer (eds.). *Verschil in Nederland - Sociaal en Cultureel Rapport 2014* (Den Haag 2014: Sociaal en Cultureel Planbureau, pp. 251-280).
The differences found in citizens' discontent can also not be explained by the divergent education levels of the various population groups. The correlation of discontent with the variable that combines the six population segments and ethnic origin is 0.42. If we control for education level, this remains substantial (0.30).

28　People with a score of 0.62 or higher were placed in the group 'high discontent'. This threshold level is equal to the value achieved by a fictitious respondent on the citizens' discontent scale, if they were to enter a 4 on all 5-point items, and an 8 on all 10-point items. The percentages do not add up to 100 because Western migrants in the insecure workers and precariat groups are not shown in the figure. They account for 6% of the discontented group.

29   Benefit dependency is theoretically a different characteristic from unemployment. The former often includes criteria other than joblessness (e.g. because poor health is a necessary condition for receiving disability benefit), while not every unemployed person is eligible for benefit. The behavioural regime generally differs depending on the type of arrangement (e.g. social assistance or unemployment insurance benefit), as do the actors and their mutual relationships. See also the models of rule-driven social security interaction in J.C. Vrooman, *Rules of Relief; Institutions of social security, and their impact* (The Hague 2009: The Netherlands Institute for Social Research|scp, pp. 143-182).

30   The following indicators were used for the network characteristics in the figure:
   – Instrumental network: number of people with an influential occupation that the person concerned knows personally (outside work), e.g. mayor, MP, managing director of a commercial company with at least 10 employees, senior civil servant, professional artist;
   – Support network, size: number of contacts with family members (outside own household), friends and close acquaintances, neighbours and local residents;
   – Support network, quality: number of people with whom the person concerned has discussed important personal issues in the last six months (excluding fellow household members and professional support workers);
   – Support network, closedness: number of people with whom the person concerned has discussed important personal issues and who know each other.

The classification as working or receiving benefit is based on the main source of income according to CBS (Statistics Netherlands) records. Excluded from the graph are Western migrants in receipt of unemployment or social assistance benefit, other benefit recipients (disability benefit, pre-pension, surviving dependants' benefit), pensioners, students and non-working people not entitled to benefit.

31   Theoretically, this can be explained by the divergent opportunities for ethnic groups to mobilise resources within the host society. Smith, for example, suggests that ethnic groups in the US do not differ only in cultural respects. Newly arrived migrants need time to build networks within their new community and generate resources within them. This puts Hispanics in the US at a disadvantage, which in turn translates into a weaker labour market position. S. S. Smith, 'Mobilizing social resources: Race, ethnic and gender differences in social capital and persisting wage inequalities', in *The Sociological Quarterly* (2000: 4, pp. 509–537).

32   There are also differences among the employed in the resources contained within their networks. Figure 5 shows that the average social capital of the established upper echelon and privileged younger people is greater than that of the employed middle echelon and insecure workers.

33   W. Huijnk, M. Gijsberts & J. Dagevos, *Jaarrapport Integratie 2013* (Den Haag 2014: Sociaal en Cultureel Planbureau); M. Gijsberts, W. Huijnk & R. Vogels (eds.), *Chinese Nederlanders; Van horeca naar hogeschool* (Den Haag 2013: Sociaal en Cultureel Planbureau).

Appendix 1 Indicators for income protection

Benefit scheme	Aspect	#	Indicator
State minimum pension	Coverage	1	Share of recipients of a non-reduced state pension
	Conditions	2	Notional insured years before introduction of state pension (1957)
	Amount	3	Guaranteed minimum income for single over-65 (disposable income, constant prices)
		4	Guaranteed minimum income for couple over-65 (disposable income, constant prices)
		5	Allowance for partner <65 years
	Duration	6	Life expectancy M/F after retirement age
Supplementary occupational pension	Coverage	7	Share of over-65s with supplementary occupational pension
	Conditions	8	Share of final salary schemes (structural income effect for standard employee)
	Amount	9	Amount of supplementary pension among recipients (constant prices)
	Duration	10	Life expectancy M/F with employment history after retirement age
Unemployment benefit	Coverage	11	Score on ladder of potential target group (18 positions)
	Conditions	12	Employment history requirements for initial earnings-related benefit
		13	Suitable employment criterion
	Amount	14	Initial benefit percentage for employees aged 25 with 5 years' employment history
		15	Initial benefit percentage for employees aged 40 with 20 years' employment history
		16	Initial benefit percentage for employees aged 58 with 38 years' employment history
		17	Average net replacement rate compared with average employee (two household types)
		18	Maximum daily wage in assessing benefit level, constant prices
	Duration	19	Maximum benefit duration for employee aged 25 with 5 years' employment history
		20	Maximum benefit duration for employee aged 40 with 20 years' employment history
		21	Maximum benefit duration for employee aged 58 with 38 years' employment history
	Reintegration	22	Reintegration budget per unemployment benefit, constant wages

Weight	Source
1.00	Sociale Verzekeringsbank
1.00	Rechtsorde database; Maxius database; De kleine gids voor de Nederlandse sociale zekerheid, 1980-2015; own calculation
0.48	Statistics Netherlands (statement)
0.48	Statistics Netherlands (statement)
0.05	Rechtsorde database; Maxius database; De kleine gids voor de Nederlandse sociale zekerheid, 1980-2015; own calculation
1.00	Statistics Netherlands; own calculation
1.00	Statistics Netherlands (Income Panel Survey)
1.00	De Nederlandsche Bank; Social and Economic Council of the Netherlands; own calculation
1.00	Statistics Netherlands (Income Panel Survey)
1.00	Statistics Netherlands; own calculation
1.00	Rechtsorde database; Maxius database; De kleine gids voor de Nederlandse sociale zekerheid, 1980-2015; own calculation
0.50	Rechtsorde database; Maxius database; De kleine gids voor de Nederlandse sociale zekerheid, 1980-2015; own calculation
0.50	Rechtsorde database; Maxius database; De kleine gids voor de Nederlandse sociale zekerheid, 1980-2015; own calculation
0.20	OECD
0.20	OECD
0.20	OECD
0.20	OECD
0.20	De kleine gids voor de Nederlandse sociale zekerheid, 1980-2015; own calculation
0.33	OECD
0.33	OECD
0.33	OECD
1.00	Ministry of Social Affairs & Employment budget; De Koning (2010); own calculation

TAKING PART IN UNCERTAINTY

Benefit scheme	Aspect	#	Indicator
Social assistance benefit	Coverage	23	Score on ladder of potential target group (18 positions)
	Conditions	24	Capital allowance (means testing), constant prices
		25	Suitable employment criterion
		26	Groups exempt from duty to work (because of age, young children, informal care obligations)
		27	Number of applicable from 10 other conditions (registration; applying for jobs; language requirements; behaviour; clothing; duty to relocate, etc.)
	Amount	28	Guaranteed minimum income for single, <65 (disposable income, constant prices)
		29	Guaranteed minimum income for couple without children, <65 (disposable income, constant prices)
		30	Guaranteed minimum income for single parent with children, <65 (disposable income, constant prices); 1-3 children
		31	Guaranteed minimum income for couple with children, <65 (disposable income, constant prices); 1-3 children
		32	Home-sharers/co-residents income norm (as % of minimum wage; average for households of 2-6 persons)
	Duration	33	Maximum number of years' regular social assistance benefit for young people aged 16-30 years
	Reintegra-tion	34	Reintegration budget per social assistance benefit, constant wages
Sick leave benefit	Coverage	35	Score on ladder of potential target group (18 positions)
	Amount	36	Average net replacement rate compared with average employee (two household types)
		37	Maximum daily wage in assessing benefit level, constant prices
	Duration	38	Maximum number of years' regular sick leave benefit
		39	Maximum number of years continued salary payment by an employer
Disability benefit	Coverage	40	Score on ladder of potential target group (18 positions)
		41	Share of sheltered employment places for disabled people as % of labour force
	Conditions	42	Incapacity for work criterion
		43	Employment history requirement for the initial earnings-related benefit in case of partial incapacity for work
		44	Means test for minimum benefit
	Amount	45	Amount of earnings-related benefit for full incapacity for work, constant prices

Weight	Source
1.00	De kleine gids voor de Nederlandse sociale zekerheid, 1980-2015
0.25	De kleine gids voor de Nederlandse sociale zekerheid, 1980-2015; own calculation
0.25	Rechtsorde database; Maxius database; De kleine gids voor de Nederlandse sociale zekerheid, 1980-2015; own calculation
0.25	Rechtsorde database; Maxius database; De kleine gids voor de Nederlandse sociale zekerheid, 1980-2015; own calculation
0.25	Rechtsorde database; Maxius database; De kleine gids voor de Nederlandse sociale zekerheid, 1980-2015; own calculation
0.20	Statistics Netherlands (statement)
0.20	Statistics Netherlands (statement)
0.20	Statistics Netherlands (statement)
0.20	Statistics Netherlands (statement)
0.20	Rechtsorde database; Maxius database; De kleine gids voor de Nederlandse sociale zekerheid, 1980-2015; own calculation
1.00	Rechtsorde database; Maxius database; De kleine gids voor de Nederlandse sociale zekerheid, 1980-2015; own calculation
1.00	Ministry of Social Affairs & Employment budget; De Koning (2010); own calculation
1.00	Rechtsorde database; Maxius database; De kleine gids voor de Nederlandse sociale zekerheid, 1980-2015; own calculation
0.50	Comparative Welfare Entitlements Dataset
0.50	De kleine gids voor de Nederlandse sociale zekerheid, 1980-2015
0.50	De kleine gids voor de Nederlandse sociale zekerheid, 1980-2015
0.50	De kleine gids voor de Nederlandse sociale zekerheid, 1980-2015
0.50	Rechtsorde database; Maxius database; De kleine gids voor de Nederlandse sociale zekerheid, 1980-2015; own calculation
0.50	Statistics Netherlands; Social and Economic Council of the Netherlands
0.33	Rechtsorde database; Maxius database; De kleine gids voor de Nederlandse sociale zekerheid, 1980-2015; own calculation
0.33	Rechtsorde database; Maxius database; De kleine gids voor de Nederlandse sociale zekerheid, 1980-2015; own calculation
0.33	Rechtsorde database; Maxius database; De kleine gids voor de Nederlandse sociale zekerheid, 1980-2015; own calculation
0.20	Kroniek van de sociale verzekeringen; own calculation

Benefit scheme	Aspect	#	Indicator
		46	Amount of earnings-related benefit for partial incapacity for work, constant prices; average over categories
		47	Amount of minimum benefit on full incapacity for work (Invalidity Benefits Act (AAW), Invalidity Provision (Early Disabled Persons) Act (Wajong), Invalidity Insurance (Self-Employed Persons) Act (WAZ)
		48	Amount of minimum benefit on partial incapacity for work; average over categories (Invalidity Benefits Act (AAW), Invalidity Provision (Early Disabled Persons) Act (Wajong), Invalidity Insurance (Self-Employed Persons) Act (WAZ)
		49	Maximum daily wage in assessing benefit level, constant prices
	Duration	50	Maximum duration for initial earnings-related benefit for non-total and non-permanent incapacity for work
Early retirement	Duration	51	Difference between official retirement age and average actual early retirement age (men)
Surviving dependants' benefit	Coverage	52	Score on ladder of potential target group (18 positions)
		53	Coverage for (semi-)orphans
	Conditions	54	Criterion for termination of benefit due to marriage or cohabitation
		55	Means test
	Amount	56	Amount of benefit for single persons with children <18
		57	Amount of benefit for single persons without children
		58	Amount of benefit for co-residents with children <18
	Duration	59	Difference between official retirement age and lower age limit for entitlement of single persons without children

Weight	Source
0.20	Kroniek van de sociale verzekeringen; own calculation
0.20	Kroniek van de sociale verzekeringen; own calculation
0.20	Kroniek van de sociale verzekeringen; own calculation
0.20	De kleine gids voor de Nederlandse sociale zekerheid, 1980-2015
1.00	CPB; Kroniek van de sociale verzekeringen; own calculation
1.00	Statistics Netherlands
0.50	Rechtsorde database; Maxius database; De kleine gids voor de Nederlandse sociale zekerheid, 1980-2015; own calculation
0.50	Sociale Verzekeringsbank
0.50	Kroniek van de sociale verzekeringen; own calculation
0.50	Kroniek van de sociale verzekeringen; own calculation
0.33	De kleine gids voor de Nederlandse sociale zekerheid, 1980-2015
0.33	De kleine gids voor de Nederlandse sociale zekerheid, 1980-2015
0.33	De kleine gids voor de Nederlandse sociale zekerheid, 1980-2015
1.00	De kleine gids voor de Nederlandse sociale zekerheid, 1980-2015

TAKING PART IN UNCERTAINTY

Appendix 2   Changing income protection in specific benefit schemes

Old age

cumulative change in income protection on scale 1-10 (1980-2015)

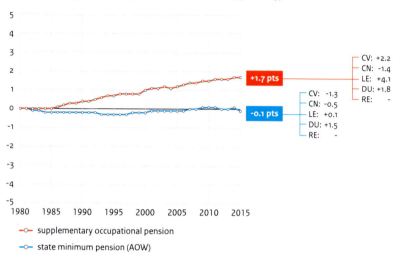

CV=coverage; CN=conditions; LE=level; DU=duration; RE=reintegration

Early retirement and death

cumulative change in income protection on scale 1-10 (1980-2015)

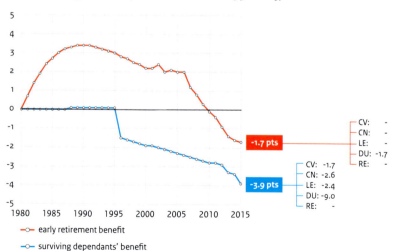

CV=coverage; CN=conditions; LE=level; DU=duration; RE=reintegration

Unemployment and social assistance

cumulative change in income protection on scale 1-10 (1980-2015)

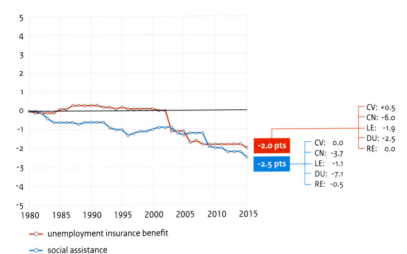

CV=coverage; CN=conditions; LE=level; DU=duration; RE=reintegration

Sick leave and disability benefit

cumulative change in income protection on scale 1-10 (1980-2015)

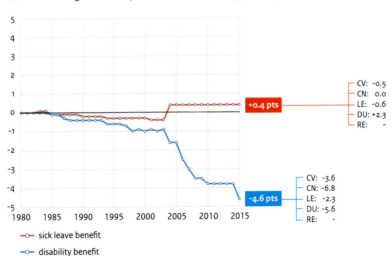

CV=coverage; CN=conditions; LE=level; DU=duration; RE=reintegration